Learning Disability in Focus

of related interest

Helping People with a Learning Disability Explore Choice
Eve and Neil Jackson
ISBN 1 85302 694 8

Helping People with a Learning Disability Explore Relationships
Eve and Neil Jackson
ISBN 1 85302 688 3

Empowerment in Everyday Life
Learning Disability
Edited by Paul Ramacharan, Gwyneth Roberts, Gordon Grant
and John Borland
ISBN 1 85302 382 5

People Skills for Young Adults
Márianna Csóti
ISBN 1 85302 716 2

Lifemaps of People with Learning Disabilities
Barry Gray and Geoff Ridden
ISBN 1 85302 690 5

Asperger's Syndrome
A Guide for Parents and Professionals
Tony Attwood
ISBN 1 85302 557 1

Learning Disability in Focus

The Use of Photography in the Care of People with a Learning Disability

Eve and Neil Jackson

Jessica Kingsley Publishers
London and Philadelphia

First published in the United Kingdom in 1999 by
Jessica Kingsley Publishers Ltd
116 Pentonville Road,
London N1 9JB, England
and
325 Chestnut Street, Philadelphia
PA 19106, USA.

www.jkp.com

Library of Congress Cataloging in Publication Data
A CIP catalog record for this book is available from the Library of Congress

British Library Cataloguing in Publication Data
Jackson, Eve
Learning disability in focus : the use of photography in the care of people with a learning disability
1. Learning disabilities – Social aspects 2. Photography in education
I. Title II. Jackson, Neil
362.2'042

ISBN 1-85302-693-X

Printed and Bound in Great Britain by
Athenaeum Press, Gateshead, Tyne and Wear

Contents

Introduction

This book is intended to serve as a practical guide to the use of photography in working with people who have a learning disability. It is born out of many years of practice and teaching, during which we have sought to help people with a learning disability to understand and control their world.

The interventions illustrated in the book will be of interest to professional nurses, social workers and other therapists, as well as informal carers. Photography can be used as an integral part of care planning or as an adjunct to existing programmes. It can be offered as a way of assisting someone with a learning disability to acquire new skills. It can help him or her to move towards an emotional well-being, and it may be influential in allaying some of the uncertainties with which that person is often faced.

The applications of photography in working with people with a learning disability are many and varied. The samples offered in this book are just some of the ways in which photography can be used to help people with a learning disability to empower themselves.

The level of use of photography in care programmes will depend upon the imagination, creativity and experience of the person implementing the programme. Its use, in particular for cathartic intervention, should be subject to supervision by a therapist who has knowledge of its implications. The users of this book will require only basic knowledge of a camera in order to use it successfully in helping people with a learning disability.

The book takes the form of a number of scenarios in which photography is used to resolve problems and enhance understanding. Each scenario is followed by a list of photographs that were used or taken in relation to the scenario. There then follows a list of useful suggestions designed to enhance the skills of the helper or carer.

The book commences with a comprehensive list of recommendations in relation to the use of photography, and ends with a summary list of important points to remember.

Recommendations for Using Photography with People who have a Learning Disability

A camera is a useful adjunct to other approaches used when working with people who have a learning disability. Below are some recommendations for when and where a camera may be used.

- In conjunction with recorded observations.

- At any stage of a task analysis or at any teaching step in an appropriate teaching programme or plan.

- To enhance understanding or to help overcome a particularly difficult step in learning.

- In any client-centred problem-solving exercise.

- In conjunction with an accepted sign, symbol or representational language system or programme.

- To reinforce learning, especially when used alongside objects involved in a teaching programme.

- To reinforce learning by combining pictures with sensations such as touch, smell and hearing.

- For choice-making, at any stage and for any level of ability.

- To aid reminiscences and to remind.

- To help someone make sense of an important event, or to act as a summary of an event.

- When exploring feelings and emotions.

- As part of a social skills programme; for example, when looking at life roles, focusing the group members, or exploring the 'self'.

- As evidence of success and achievement.

- To help someone through the grieving process.

- To give information and help prepare someone prior to an outing, activity or unexpected event.

- When creating a 'tailor made' programme designed to move a person towards a more independent life-style.

- At an early stage of a desensitization programme.

- As a new leisure skill to be mastered.

- To give immediate feedback after a meaningful event; for example, a trip to the hairdresser's.

Case Studies

Laura

Laura is 13 years old and lives at home with her parents, two younger brothers, a younger sister and one older brother. Life at home is at times a bit chaotic and sometimes Laura misses out on some of the individual attention from which she would benefit.

Laura enjoys attending the local special school. It gives her the structure and routine which seems to be lacking from her home life.

Laura lacks confidence and her teacher realizes that this must be partly due to Laura's poor memory. However, Laura excels at art and craft-work and has in the past produced some good drawings, needlework and pottery. Sadly, this is not always appreciated at home and Laura's achievements have not always received the attention they deserve. Laura always insists 'Show Mum', even though this generally means that the work is 'lost' at home and so is not available for display on the school's Open Day.

Recently, Laura's teacher found herself spending more and more time prompting and encouraging Laura before she would begin on a new art activity. Laura's confidence seemed very low indeed.

Laura's teacher needed to find a way of reminding Laura of what she had achieved in the past. She hoped that this would help Laura to regain her loss of confidence, and make it easier for her to undertake a new project.

Laura's teacher used photography as an aid. She encouraged Laura to look at pictures of the art and craft-work that she had produced over the past term. She began each new activity by praising Laura for her past accomplishments. This had the desired effect, and soon Laura had regained some of her confidence and was more willing to try a new activity when it was offered.

In future, whatever happens at home to her original work, Laura will always have her pictures as proof of her achievements.

Photographs were taken of:

- Laura preparing for an activity.
- Laura doing the activity.
- The completed work.
- Each completed piece of art and craft-work.
- The end-of-term Open Day.
- Awards, certificates etc. which Laura won.

Remember to:

- Label and date each photograph clearly. Keep them all in an album.
- Give your pupil time to look at photographs before a new activity is begun.
- Praise and encourage your pupil to acknowledge work done.
- Discuss your pupil's achievements with his or her parents or guardians.
- Consider other pupils, who may be experiencing different problems, that this approach may also suit.

Mr Bates

Mr Bates is a 72-year-old gentleman who lives in a residential care home.

Mr Bates suffers from a quite severe loss of hearing, and, although physically active, he can become confused if anxious about anything. This results in Mr Bates resolutely refusing to do anything or go anywhere.

Mr Bates often needs to attend various appointments, such as with his GP at the nearby surgery, at the out-patients clinic at the local hospital, at the hearing-aid clinic and with the chiropodist. Because of the variety of appointments and different destinations, it is important that the staff working in the home inform Mr Bates accurately, so that he is able to prepare himself for any outings or visits.

Staff put together a collection of photographs of all the places Mr Bates visited regularly. These were used as a way of preparing Mr Bates prior to an outing. They showed him where he was going, whom he would be likely to see, what would be happening.

As a result, Mr Bates appeared calmer and more accepting of any appointments that he needed to attend.

Photographs were taken of:

- Entrances to clinics, surgeries and the hospital. Signs, symbols and names Mr Bates would encounter.

- Waiting areas and reception areas.

- Clinical areas and appointment rooms.

- Doctors, nurses, the chiropodist and the audiologist.

- Mr Bates being treated on a previous visit.

- Mr Bates shaking hands and leaving the clinics.

- The transport used to take Mr Bates to appointments.

Remember to:

- Place each set of photographs of the activity or outing in a separate folder or album to eliminate confusion.

- Label photographs clearly.

- Give the person time – taking his or her own pace – to look at and assimilate the information from the photographs.

- 'Talk through' the photographs as and when appropriate.

- Be aware that someone's anxiety linked to going out, or more specifically to any of the individual appointments, may be expressed in any number of ways.

- Offer time and support to help overcome fears and concerns.

Sarah

Sarah, aged ten, lives in a home owned by the local social services. A large number of staff work at the home, some full-time, others part-time; with shifts alternating from early to late duty on a weekly rota. In addition, the night staff work three nights on and four nights off, and extra staff are employed to work just weekends across all shifts. Holidays and sickness is usually covered by staff working overtime, but sometimes it has been necessary to use relief or 'bank' staff.

Sarah knows a good many of the staff and has her own personal (key) member of staff who tries to give her extra time, is aware of her individual needs and co-ordinates her care.

Sarah enjoys attending the local special school and has never exhibited any particular behaviour problems. Recently, however, Sarah became noisy and started to bring attention to herself towards the end of the school day. As nothing at school appeared to be triggering Sarah's behaviour, her teacher first checked with the driver and attendant on the school bus, and then consulted with the home staff. The staff didn't know of any incidents or any particular reason which would cause Sarah to become so upset.

It seemed that Sarah was reluctant to leave school at the end of the day and was unwilling to tell anyone why.

Over the next three weeks, Sarah's behaviour worsened and she began spitting at her classmates and those with whom she travelled home on the bus. Then one day Sarah refused to leave the bus and burst into tears. In between sobs and hanging on to the seat she asked:

'Who's at home? Is it someone new?'

Enquiries were made, and it was established that the turn-over of staff had been particularly high recently. The members of staff with whom Sarah was most familiar were having to change duties, and new, unfamiliar faces were being introduced all the time. In fact, the place that had always offered Sarah the most security and safety was now causing her to feel unsettled, disrupted and unsafe. Sarah no longer had any idea who would be there to greet her when she arrived home from school, or how her routine would differ. She had no way of preparing herself: her behaviour was a reaction to this and a way of avoiding any more disappointment.

Sarah's key member of staff decided to introduce photographs as a way of informing Sarah who would be coming on duty and when.

All the staff at the home produced photographs of themselves – including occasional staff – and these were displayed so that the children could familiarize themselves with those members of staff with whom they had only minimal contact.

Photographs were taken of:

- All staff members.
- Members of staff whom Sarah related to a particular activity.

Remember to:

- Display photographs in conjunction with a calendar or timetable, to illustrate when staff are coming on duty (i.e, breakfast-time, after dinner, after school).

- Change the display daily if necessary.

- Talk to the child about who is on duty for the day/night, making this part of a regular routine.

- Consider whether it may be appropriate for the child to carry a photograph in his or her school bag. This may enable the teacher to remind him or her who is on duty.

- Contact the school, if sudden staff changes are unavoidable, so that the child is not disappointed or confused.

- Share with the school any changes at the home or in the child's behaviour, and remember that continuity of approach is essential for any programme of care to work.

- Meet the child's needs regarding feelings of safety, and recognize the role staff need to play in developing and communicating that sense of security in a way that is appropriate to that child.

Les

Les is 47 years old and his mother has just died.

His father died when he was a baby and therefore Les has no recollection of him.

Les shares a house with three other men, who, like him, will always require a high level of support.

Les had been visited by his mother twice a week for many years. Staff realized that Les would miss his mother not only for the love and friendship she always gave him, but for the routine of her visits that had proved to be a source of comfort and stability to him.

Staff were aware of the importance of involving Les at every stage of the funeral arrangements and were sensitive to his needs throughout. Kathy, the member of staff who was closest to Les, accompanied Les to his mother's funeral. Two distant relatives also attended, but the concept of being 'related' did not mean anything to Les. Friends and neighbours were there in abundance: Les recognized some of his mother's neighbours and seemed pleased to see them. One of the neighbours handed Les a photograph of his mother taken the previous summer. Les held on to this photograph and refused to put it down, still carrying it around with him some days later.

Kathy understood this need for Les to 'hold on' to his mother. She had decided to take some photographs of the funeral to help

Les through his bereavement. She included photographs of the church, the flowers, the people who attended and the vicar.

Kathy had decided that photographs would be the focal point for Les at those times of the week when his mother would normally have visited him. Initially, she placed the photographs at the front of an album and Les concentrated on only these at first. Les repeated his questions over and over again, and Kathy spent this time sitting with Les and helping him make some sense of what had happened. Each time he opened the album he became upset and cried. Kathy realized that Les needed this time of grieving and helped him to cry. But as time passed Kathy noticed that Les was spending less and less time on the first pages in the album, and was quickly moving on to the photographs which represented happier memories for him; pictures of him and his mother having fun together. Kathy used this as a way to measure Les's progress through the bereavement process.

She decided that it was time to gather up the photographs that reminded him of the funeral and place them in an envelope. She returned the envelope to the album, giving Les the choice of looking at the photographs rather than be faced with them every time he opened the album. Les appeared to appreciate this. Kathy then began to look at ways of introducing new interests and activities into Les's life, to help fill, in some small way, the gap left by his mother's death.

Photographs were taken of:

- The church.

- The flowers and wreaths.

- Friends and relatives.

- The vicar.

- Les's early family life.

- Holidays, visits, outings Les took with his mother.

- Recent occasions when Les and his mother were together.

Remember to:

- Arrange the photographs in sequence in an album.

- Use the photographs as a focal point when talking through the grieving process.

- Make available photographs that will give comfort and act as reminders of happy times.

- Put together an album of friends, past acquaintances and even members of staff who have left the home. Loss isn't always about someone dying.

- Use photographs as a memory jogger and to encourage communication at any point, not just in times of crisis.

College Students

Staff at a further education unit were introducing a 'Learning To Cope' programme for students who needed to acquire skills in finding and using their local community resources. The first term was used to look at local amenities and how to find them. As part of this course, the students were taught simple map-making, starting with a map of the college itself.

From this the students then acquainted themselves with the town map and the local bus routes. When the group moved on to discuss the local amenities, staff used existing pictures of typical buildings – such as the library, school, police station and job centre – to enable the students to familiarize themselves with these places. It soon became apparent, however, that some of the students were having difficulty with this.

After some discussion it was discovered that the pictures were not a sufficiently true likeness: they did not represent accurately, for some, the buildings they saw in their own town.

It was decided that the members of the group would make their own collection of pictures by photographing places, buildings and amenities that were known to them. The students enjoyed the personal involvement of creating something that could be used by future college students. Later, they took on a project to create 'maps' with the use of photographs, which were for those students less able than themselves. This included making personal journey maps. These could enable students to get to know the college areas better, or to help them find the shops and buildings located in their own vicinity.

Photographs were taken of:

- Buildings and amenities with a sign clearly indicating their names or numbers.

- Signposts or cues.

- Views of streets.

- College corridors, doors, signs, arrows etc.

Remember to:

- Use photographs as a basis for discussion, for example, 'Where is it?' 'How do I find it?' 'What do I use it for?' 'How often do I visit that building?'

- Use photography when creating a 'map' or guide to help a person towards independent shopping or visiting places within the locality.

- Introduce gradually similar pictures of buildings from other towns and cities, so that students will learn to generalize their knowledge and skills.

- Place photographs in a small album or easily-managed folder, named and labelled for each separate destination.

Brian

Brian is 17 years old and lives at home with his parents.

He attends college three days a week and enjoys his Wednesday cookery class particularly.

Recently, Brian has indicated to his parents that he wishes to practise cooking at home, so that one day he will be able to cook a family meal. Up until now Brian has only prepared his own breakfast and made his own cups of tea and coffee at home, preferring to confine any new cooking skills to the familiar surroundings of the college kitchen. This wish to practise at home was seen as quite a breakthrough for Brian who, while always enjoying any new independence, still lacked self-confidence.

Brian's community nurse arranged for Brian to borrow a set of cookery cards from the 'special needs' section of the college library. One set of cards illustrated the ingredients and the kitchen utensils required, another, the methods to be used for a number of recipes. Brian had already been successful in using these at college. His mother would be on hand to assist if he needed her.

When the community nurse called the following week to see how Brian had got on, she was surprised to hear that Brian had been unable to cope with cooking at home and had even lost his temper.

The community nurse suggested to Brian that he cook something while she was there to help. This would give her the opportunity to observe and possibly to identify the problem. She wondered whether Brian's mother had offered too much assistance!

The nature of the problem soon became clear. The picture cards that Brian was using did not clearly represent the foods and utensils in his mum's kitchen. They just didn't match up. For instance, while one picture card showed an electrical whisk, Brian's mum only had a hand whisk – Brian knew how to use this but not where she kept it. The jug was a different shape and colour to the pictured jug, and foods were stored in containers. The subtle differences were enough to confuse Brian and make him feel anxious and unsure of himself.

The community nurse suggested that it might be better if Brian had his own 'tailor-made' set of cards for use at home. This set of cards would match his mum's kitchen and contents perfectly, and he wouldn't have to give them back to the library when the loan expired.

Brian's dad took this on gladly and soon the whole family was involved. Each cooking task was broken down into small steps that Brian could understand, and photographed. Photographs were also taken of the foodstuffs and utensils involved at each stage. The photographs formed the basis of the new cards.

The idea worked so well that Brian's dad then went on to make Brian a set of cards for laying the table.

Photographs were taken of:

- Each individual kitchen utensil required.

- The ingredients needed.

- Storage jars and containers.

- The layout of the kitchen, i.e. cupboards, fridge, oven.

- Techniques used (e.g. whisking, mixing, greasing of pans) and general instructions such as hands being washed.

- The completed dish.

Remember to:

- Observe the person first to ascertain skill level and steps required.

- Place the photographs in a plastic sleeve or laminate them to protect them.

- Arrange the photographs in the correct sequence.

- Try presenting other independent living skills in this way, such as bathing, dressing, and packing a school bag.

Miss Williams

Miss Williams is 61 years old and shares a house close to the town centre with four other adults.

Miss Williams is at times a little unsteady on her feet and sometimes uses a walking frame, which she doesn't like.

Miss Williams is fiercely independent, and although the other residents are younger and more physically active, she insists on 'doing her bit' around the house. She is also rather forgetful and this, combined with her wish to be independent, began to create arguments between her and the other residents. Miss Williams constantly forgot which household task she had agreed to do and would switch her attention to someone else's job. When another resident pointed out that she had made a mistake, she would argue and insist that he or she was in the wrong. If a member of staff tried to explain or remind her she became agitated and flustered, lost her concentration and became in danger of falling.

Staff needed a way of reminding Miss Williams which task she had agreed to do and what it involved, but one which offered her an element of self-control so that she was not continually relying on others.

Photographs were used as a way of offering Miss Williams a choice of task and then as a prompt. She carried the photographs around in her pocket and used them to remind herself what she should be doing. Miss Williams really appreciated the independence this offered her, and confrontation with other residents and members of staff was eliminated.

Photographs were taken of:

- An object which represented a task, e.g. furniture polish and duster, vacuum cleaner.

- The room or area specific to each task.

- Objects representing weekend and leisure activities.

Remember to:

- Present photographs when offering a choice of tasks each day.

- Offer photographs as a reminder of weekend activities.

- Use in conjunction with diaries or timetables if appropriate.

- Make a chart of tasks which a client can tick off on completion.

- Always praise and identify the specific task completed.

Liam

Liam is fourteen and lives at home with his parents and his nine-year-old sister Melanie, and is very much a part of a loving family.

Although Liam is confined to a wheelchair and has minimal verbal communication, he is involved wherever possible in all family outings and activities. He is alert, with a good sense of humour, and enjoys lots of company.

Liam had always found going out an adventure, so much so that he often needed calming before his coat and boots could be put on. Although his initial enthusiasm never waned, his family were becoming aware of a change in his behaviour when they arrived at their destination. Usually he became sullen and quiet, but one evening, in the middle of his sister's dance rehearsal, he began to rage and shout. Melanie was embarrassed at his behaviour and the attention it brought, and asked if Liam could stay at home in future.

This outburst of Liam's was to be one of many similar scenes and the family were naturally concerned at his apparent unhappiness. After some discussion they decided that as Liam was now in his teens his behaviour was possibly a way of demanding some independence from them. They realized that trailing after his mother and younger sister was probably not much fun for Liam any more.

So, his dad decided to take him out more often, and began to introduce him to some new activities in which he might take an interest.

Liam greeted the opportunity of even more outings with his usual enthusiasm, but still, on arriving he would be full of misery, rocking his wheelchair and groaning.

It was purely by chance that his sister Melanie stumbled upon the reason for Liam's outbursts. His mum was getting him ready to go to the shops when Melanie approached him and asked: 'Where are you off to, then?' Liam began to moan and wail.

His mum answered for him: 'The shops, aren't we Liam? Here, you hold the shopping bag.'

This immediately quietened Liam.

After a similar incident, his mum realized that Liam became upset when he did not know where he was going: not every outing was accompanied by such an obvious cue as a shopping bag. She suspected that Liam was often disappointed once he had arrived at his destination. She had been unable to convey to Liam the information he required in order to prepare himself to go somewhere, or to give him a choice of whether or not he actually wanted to go.

The family worked together to help Liam. Melanie enjoyed gathering objects to use as cues, and her dad put together a collection of photographs that would give Liam the information he needed to make choices.

With these photographs, Liam was soon choosing his own weekend activities in keeping with his age and development. His parents saw this as real progress. Liam was also saved the frustration of not knowing where he was going and finding himself, without warning, somewhere he didn't wish to be.

Photographs were taken of:

- Familiar activities or destinations.

- New activities or destinations.

- Objects or tools associated with certain activities.

- Particular areas or rooms associated with certain activities.

Remember to:

- Build up choice-making skills gradually.

- Use objects as cues to help someone make the link with the activity: for example, a picture of a bathing costume and towel before a trip to the swimming pool.

- Ensure that the activity follows the selected choice.

- Involve others, especially siblings, whenever possible, and be imaginative.

Maria

Maria, aged 23, lives in a group home. Although Maria is confined to a wheelchair she values her independence and is involved in various groups and local activities.

One of her favourite activities is attending an art and craft workshop once a week. In the past Maria has attempted most of the practical workshops on offer, from jewellery-making to pottery, and watercolour painting to picture framing. There is no doubt that Maria has an artistic eye, but she has never been quite able to translate her ideas into practice. Maria's spasticity restricted her arm and hand movements, and even with assistance the finished product never met with her approval. She knew if too much 'help' was being offered and would reject work immediately as not being her own.

Maria's tutor was aware of Maria's growing disappointment, and was afraid that she would give up art and craftwork altogether. He realized that Maria needed to attain a level of competence in art that satisfied her, and a one that did not continually face her with her disability and its many restrictions.

Maria was offered the opportunity to join the photography class. It was hoped that with some initial assistance and on-going support when needed, Maria would be able to cope with a basic photography course and put her artistic talents to good use.

Maria started off with a camera that gave her 'instant' results. Before long, she realized that if she wanted to produce better quality pictures then she would have to wait for the results. She moved on to a compact automatic with an in-built zoom lens. The controls were easy to handle and the camera was light to hold.

With her tutor's help, Maria was soon able to distinguish between a good and a not-so-good photograph. Her confidence grew and she became more and more imaginative with her shots. Her camera went everywhere with her as she began to understand just how much photography offered her. She had discovered a new and exciting dimension to her world.

Photographs were taken of:

- Cameras and examples of the types of picture which they were capable of producing.

- Examples of lighting, angles etc. that worked/didn't work.

WITHDRAWN

Remember to:

- Purchase or borrow a good illustrated book of photography as a way of introducing the subject, and to show what is possible.

- Try out various cameras to find one that suits.

- Find out whether remote switches, tripods or any auxiliary equipment would be helpful.

- Experiment with enlarging and reducing photographs.

- Frame successful pictures so that they can be better appreciated.

- Give plenty of opportunity to use a camera in different and imaginative situations.

- Arrange a visit to a photography exhibition.

- Consider establishing a dark room to develop your own pictures.

- Help the person explore all avenues; if his or her work is good, arrange a local exhibition of work. Look out for local group activities such as holidays designed for those with an interest in photography. Is the work good enough to be sold?

Patrick

Patrick is seven years old and is preparing to go on holiday to the seaside for the first time in his life.

Although Patrick has limited verbal communication, he is a lively and enthusiastic little boy who works extremely hard at being understood.

Bill, Patrick's helper, knew that Patrick would be eager to share everything about his adventures on his return. He decided to photograph the whole event in some detail. Not only would this provide Patrick with some holiday snapshots of his activities, which he could show others, it would also form a complete record of this important event in Patrick's life. Bill hoped that Patrick would be able to use the photographs as a reminder in years to come, and that it would serve as a useful tool to help him make more sense of the whole idea of 'going on holiday'.

Photographs were taken of:

- Pictures from brochures.

- Patrick packing his suitcase.

- The transport used.

- Patrick leaving for his holiday.

- Landmarks seen *en route.*

- Stops on the way.

- Holiday accommodation.

- Activities enjoyed during the holiday.

- Places visited.

- Friends met on holiday.

- New foods tried.

- Purchases.

- The whole group who went on holiday together.

Remember to:

- Use photographs you have taken in conjunction with pictures from holiday brochures and postcards.

- Store photographs in a strong, well-bound album – it's likely to be well-thumbed!

- Place them in sequence, and label and date them.

- Include other items such as tickets and programmes.

- Write a simple account of the holiday.

- Keep the negatives safe to replace the photographs if necessary.

Social Skills Group

Staff at the day centre were planning their next set of social skills groups.

The aims were:

- to help members of the group to be aware of their facial expressions, body language and gestures, and the part that these play in their interactions with others

- to encourage group members to acknowledge their own feelings and emotions through honest, open discussion, and to promote a deeper level of understanding of the 'self'.

Having recently evaluated their last group, the staff were aware that some changes were necessary. Interest amongst the members of that group had waned; because of this the staff decided that, rather than use the all too-familiar package of 'social skill' cards, they would help the students to produce their own pictures which would form the basis of their discussions.

By using photographs of the students themselves, the staff hoped to bring about an element of personal involvement. This, in turn, would renew interest within the group and also focus on the members' thoughts and feelings.

Photographs illustrating different facial expressions, gestures and body positions were discussed and interpreted. Role play, which offered members the opportunity to 'act out' and put into context the emotions portrayed in the photographs, was enjoyed. Ideas on clothes, accessories and general presentation were also debated.

Members were paired off to discuss their experiences and associated feelings; this included how they presented themselves to others and how they really felt inside.

Discussions on how assumptions are made and confusions arise led on to a more confrontational style of group interaction. The group as a whole was more open with its disclosures than previous groups had been, and this allowed group members and facilitators to understand each other's viewpoints.

On the whole, there was a greater commitment to the group than in previous years, and this resulted in members gaining in confidence and becoming more aware of others. The unexpected bonus was that by using their own photographs – some of which were good, others not quite so good – they introduced an element of humour which was enjoyed by everyone!

Photographs were taken of:

- Each group member, including facilitators/leaders.

- Facial expressions, showing a range of emotions.

- Body language in different settings.

- Group members dressed for different occasions/moods.

- Old photographs that evoke a strong feeling/emotion.

Remember to:

- Use photographs as a way of making any social skills group more personal, and as a way of helping to establish group cohesiveness and ownership of the group.

- Try photographs specifically to explore the 'self' incorporating the role of body language, facial expressions and gestures.

- Use as a starting point for understanding and learning new skills through role play.

- Include photographs of group leaders or facilitators; this will give members the opportunity to see a face other than the one presented in the work role. It may also offer a new direction for discussion on 'life' roles'.

Joy

Joy is 52 years old and has recently moved into a flat shared by two other ladies. The flat is close to the town centre and is Joy's first real home away from an institutional setting in which she has lived since her early childhood.

Staff anticipated that Joy would be anxious and would need some time to adjust to this huge change in her lifestyle. They were also aware that Joy has a problem retaining new information and they did everything possible to alleviate any confusion that Joy might experience. Prior to moving in, Joy was given the opportunity to meet and get to know the ladies with whom she would be sharing the flat. Joy was given a photograph of them to remind her and help her 'know' them better.

The flat was in a new building, and Joy had 'seen' it being built through a succession of photographs taken at every stage of construction. By the time that Joy moved in, she felt that she knew the flat well. This was important to her: she needed to be familiar with her surroundings before she could settle in and relax.

On moving in, Joy was given photographs of friends, staff and even pictures of the old wards she had left behind. These she placed in a large album which served both as a reminder and as a reminiscence diary.

Joy has developed a network of friends over the years including hospital volunteers, church members and ladies she had met at the local music appreciation group. She was encouraged to keep photographs of each function, meeting or activity in which she was involved. These were marked underneath with the day, date and time she usually attended. She kept these out where she could see them to remind herself of her weekly commitments.

During the settling-in period Joy had new names and faces to get to know. Staff helped by bringing in photographs of themselves with their names attached and pinning these up on a notice board in the kitchen. Joy seemed to appreciate this and was often seen checking the board in the mornings and memorizing names.

As Joy has become more settled, staff have begun to build up a small library of photographs that would help her in the future. These include people that she may need to visit in the future, including the GP, dentist, hairdresser etc. and unfamiliar places such as local shops, the post office and the library. When each new photograph is added, staff sit and talk through the pictures with Joy to explore any problems or particular anxieties that she may have, prior to exploring her new environment.

Photographs were taken of:

- The flat during construction.
- Friends and acquaintances.
- Past activities.
- Former living accommodation and familiar areas.
- New staff and friends.
- On-going activities and groups.
- People whom Joy needed to get to know.
- Places which Joy may visit in the future.

Remember to:

- Place photographs in sequence of events, and label them clearly.
- Use a 'calendar' with the photographs as a reminder of meetings, appointments, etc.
- Use a notice board to 'advertise' new staff or unfamiliar faces that the person may need to know.
- Offer to frame significant photographs to acknowledge their importance in your client's life. It should be their choice – not yours!
- Use photographs as a focus for discussing anxieties or concerns about a subject or place. Or even as a part of an agreed desensitisation programme.

A Practical Guide to the Use of Photography in a Training Programme

The purpose of this chapter is to draw together the techniques of using photography with people who have a learning disability explored in the rest of the book, and to illustrate them through a training programme.

This chapter outlines the training of Bill and discusses it in relation to the development of a new skill.

Bill

Bill is 32 years old and lives in a staffed group home on the outskirts of a small seaside town. He shares it with two other people.

Although Bill has a learning disability he is able to comprehend many things that are said to him and he has a limited range of verbal communication. He has developed ways of communicating through the use of a sign language (Makaton) and through the use of gestures.

His parents and his brother live in the same town as Bill and have been very supportive of his move into the staffed group home. His parents are getting older now and have become somewhat frail: they feel that Bill needs to be with younger people, and are very satisfied with the care that he has received in the group home.

Bill is a very inquisitive, and at times assertive man, who enjoys most of his weekly activities such as going to the day centre where he works with his friend David, shopping, assisting with the cooking of meals and watching television with the others in the house.

Bill's journey

The aim of Bill's programme is to help him to use public transport (the bus) independently to get from his home to the day centre that he attends during the week. At the moment Bill travels to the centre on the bus with one of his carers, or by minibus with other people from the centre; the most frequently-used form of transport is the bus. Bill seems to enjoy the journey whichever form of transport is used and likes arriving at the centre. He also seems to be motivated to return 'home' at the end of the day.

Training programme

The assessment phase

The first phase of his training is to be supervised by a community nurse for people with a learning disability, and responsibility for the care will then be delegated in the second phase to one of the health care assistants who works with Bill in his home.

The community nurse uses a global or holistic approach to the assessment of Bill and his attendance at the centre. It is important for her to discover what Bill can understand and do already in order to develop new knowledge and skills. Photographs can be used at this stage to make a record of aspects of Bill's life and work; see for example, Photographs A and B.

Photograph A: Bill working hard

Subject: Bill at work at the day centre focusing on a positive aspect of his work and showing him smiling and busy.

The photograph must be clear and Bill must be clearly recognizable in it.

This photograph will be used to reinforce Bill's achievements at the centre and as a reminder of his destination while he is undertaking the journey by bus.

Photograph B: Bill and friends at the day centre

Subject: Bill and his friends at the day centre, perhaps when they are taking a break in the canteen.

This photograph will help to remind Bill, and those who care for him, that working at the centre is a significant part of his life and the goal of getting there independently is important.

It can also be referred to when asking Bill how his friends get to work.

It will be important during the assessment phase to make a photographic record of Bill's journey as it is *currently* undertaken. This record can be used as a pictorial **baseline** against which future development can be measured and progress seen clearly by all, including, of course, Bill. The person taking the photographs needs to be sensitive to and respectful of Bill's needs, and should have the basic techniques of photography. Photographs used in the assessment phase can be used later to demonstrate the progression that has been made from dependent to independent travel; see, for example, Photograph C.

Photograph C: Bill on his way

Subject: Bill getting ready to go to work accompanied by one of his carers.

This photograph needs to record the fact that Bill needs help to get to work.

The photograph, however, must not demean Bill in any way.

Ensure that Bill and the minibus are all clearly visible in the shot. As in all photographs for use in this project, take several shots and select the one that best illustrates the scene.

Aim

The main aim of the training programme is to promote Bill's autonomy and independence in relation to his daily travel. However, subsidiary aims may be generated, for example:

- increasing confidence;

- increasing competence;

- increasing self awareness;

- developing the ability to reflect on the past and to acknowledge past achievements;

- extending Bill's new travel skills to other areas of his life, for example, visiting David, going to the cinema, going shopping.

Photographs used in the assessment phase (A–D) can be used later to compare the effectiveness of the new form of travel with that of old ones; for example, see Photograph D.

Photograph D: The minibus in heavy traffic

Subject: Photograph showing the minibus outside a house, door open, waiting for another client.

Bill should be clearly visible in the photograph but the main point to illustrate is that he is not getting to work very quickly.

This photograph emphasizes the fact that the minibus can sometimes be a slow and inefficient way for Bill and his carer to travel.

The assessment phase will also be concerned with Bill's understanding of the key steps in learning how to use a bus to get to the centre, for example:

- basic money recognition (with assistance);

- travelcard purchase (with assistance initially);

- recall of journey through the recognition of key landmarks, using photographs to aid memory;

- use of bus timetable;

- use of bus (initially with assistance, but this will be gradually withdrawn over time).

Having assessed Bill's current level of functioning in relation to travel and work the community nurse, in conjunction with Bill and his carers, will use the photographs already taken alongside additional ones to reinforce what he has learned.

The action phase

The carer should:

- Take Bill to the centre on the Number 29 bus.

- Use the photographs of Bill at the centre (A and B) to reinforce the destination.

- Use photographs of the journey (1–9) to establish and reinforce Bill's recognition of key landmarks on the journey.

- Check Bill's recognition of landmarks using photographs as cues in the form of a quiz, for example, the carer could ask: 'What have we just passed, Bill?' and show a choice of two photographs. It is important that the carer remembers to praise Bill when he gets it right.

- Gradually withdraw from accompanying Bill on the journey in the following way:

WEEK ONE

Accompany Bill for the whole journey, using Photographs 1–9 to establish Bill's recognition of the chosen landmarks.

WEEK TWO

Accompany Bill until the bus reaches the stop before the centre, check with Bill that he knows that he gets off at the next stop, and reinforce this using Photograph 9. The carer should alight.

SUBSEQUENT WEEKS

The carer should continue to withdraw at successive bus stops, as agreed in discussion with the community nurse and Bill, until Bill is completing the journey on his own.

It is important to follow up the programme by checking periodically (by accompanying Bill on his journey and allowing him to take the lead in describing landmarks and announcing the stop at which to alight) to check that the learning is well-established.

The photographs used to establish Bill's recognition of the journey through the use of landmarks

These photographs should be put into a 'flip' wallet for Bill to take with him each day, and as he understands numbers they should be clearly numbered 1–9. A spare similar wallet should be kept at home with copies of the photographs numbered in exactly the same way, in case the original wallet is mislaid.

Photograph 1: Bill purchasing his travelcard

Subject: Bill getting his travelcard from the bus station in the town, handing over money and receiving the card in exchange.

This photograph will be used to remind Bill that he needs to get a new travelcard each month and also of his growing skills and independence.

Photograph 2: Bill boarding the Number 29 bus at the stop he will use every day

Subject: Bill just at the point where he gets on the bus. The photograph must clearly show the number of the bus, and detail of the area around the bus stop.

This photograph will be used to help Bill to recognize his bus and discriminate it from others and recognise the stop at which he catches the bus, it will also be useful in reinforcing his achievement in the early stages of the programme.

Photograph 3: Bill using his travelcard on the bus

Subject: Bill putting his card into the machine on the bus, perhaps also interacting with the bus driver.

This photograph will be used to remind Bill that he needs to have his travelcard with him at all times in his wallet, and that his ability to do things independently is growing.

Photograph 4: The supermarket

Subject: the supermarket. The photograph must be taken from the angle at which Bill would see it from the bus.

This photograph will be used to rehearse and reinforce Bill's ability to recognize his journey, in conjunction with photographs of other landmarks.

The photograph can also be used at other times when asking Bill to choose between activities such as *shopping* and *going to the park* (see Photograph 5).

Photograph 5: The park

Subject: the park as it would be seen from the bus. Photographing the park as the bus approaches it and then again after the bus has gone past creates an impression of movement and could be developed into a more complex landmark series.

This photograph will be used to rehearse and reinforce Bill's ability to recognize his journey, in conjunction with photographs of other landmarks.

The photograph can also be used at other times when asking Bill to choose between activities such as *going to the park,* or *going to the bank* (see Photograph 6).

Photograph 6: Bill's bank

Subject: the bank, as it would be seen from the bus.

This photograph will be used to rehearse and reinforce Bill's ability to recognize his journey, in conjunction with photographs of other landmarks.

The photograph can also be used at other times when asking Bill to choose between activities such as *going to the bank* or *going to the cinema* (see Photograph 7).

Photograph 7: The cinema

Subject: the cinema as it would be seen from the bus.

This photograph will be used to rehearse and reinforce Bill's ability to recognize his journey in conjunction with photographs of other landmarks.

The photograph can also be used at other times when asking Bill to choose between activities such as *going to the cinema* or *going to visit David* (see Photograph 8).

Photograph 8: David's house

Subject: David's house as it would be viewed from the bus. It would help to include David in the photograph waving to Bill.

This photograph will be used to rehearse and reinforce Bill's ability to recognize his journey, in conjunction with photographs of other landmarks.

The photograph can also be used at other times when asking Bill to choose between activities such as *visiting David* or *going to the supermarket* (see Photograph 4).

Photograph 9: The centre

Subject: the centre where Bill works. The photograph should show the entrance that Bill normally uses and could include Bill walking in to the entrance with a friend.

This photograph will be used to rehearse and reinforce Bill's ability to recognize his journey, in conjunction with photographs of other landmarks.

Evaluation phase

In the evaluation phase the community nurse calls together all those people who have been involved in the programme, including Bill, of course, and perhaps his parents, who have taken a keen interest in his developing autonomy. A number of questions are asked:

- Has the main aim of the programme been met?

- Have any subsidiary aims been met?

- Have any general issues in relation to Bill's care emerged that need to be addressed?

- Can it be judged that Bill is now getting to work safely as well as independently?

- Are there any resource implications in relation to the programme – what did it cost, what benefits have been accrued?

- Are there any outstanding concerns in relation to Bill's travel?

The evaluation meeting

Bill's carer reported to the evaluation meeting that Bill succeeded in getting to work independently within eight weeks of the commencement of the programme. A problem did occur in that the carer felt she withdrew too quickly and on one occasion Bill got off at the wrong stop. A member of staff from the centre saw him and things were resolved, but the incident did reduce Bill's confidence. The carer then started accompanying Bill again and withdrew more slowly, taking her lead from Bill.

The community nurse felt that the programme had gone very well despite the setback outlined by the carer, which she felt was just the first step in developing increased autonomy for Bill. She complimented Bill on his success and thanked the carer and the manager of the centre for their help and support.

Bill expressed his pleasure at achieving his goal and also thanked those involved. He said to the meeting that it was *'nice doing it on my own'.*

Bill's parents were pleased with his progress. They expressed concern at the incident where Bill got off at the wrong stop but were glad that the community nurse had talked this through with them at the time. They were happy to be included in the programme and thanked all concerned for taking the time to help Bill develop a new skill.

The people at the meeting went on to discuss coping strategies should something go wrong. They brainstormed some of the possibilities with a 'what if' sheet;

What if…

- The bus did not run because of mechanical failure or bad weather?

- The bus was late?

- There was a diversion from the normal route caused by road works?

- The number of the route was changed?

A strategy would have to be devised to deal with each one of these possibilities. The carer agreed to give this some thought and liaise with the community nurse regarding solutions. Bill told the group that the bus had been late some days, and that other people who were waiting at his stop told him that it would 'be along in a minute or two'. The people at the meeting were pleased that Bill was learning many things as a consequence of the programme.

The meeting concluded with Bill suggesting that, now he can use the bus he might visit David one Saturday on his own. Everyone agreed that this was a good idea and a useful next step, and his carer agreed to start to plan for this to happen.

Discussion

The study of Bill and his journey to work has illustrated the ways in which photography can be used to enhance a training programme. In the examples given in the previous chapters a similar process would be undertaken. The process of the incorporation of photography into care or training can be encapsulated in the steps below:

1. Assess the person's current behaviours given the situation.

2. Identify aspects of the situation in which a photograph would help to illustrate a concept.

   For example, Liam (page 37) did not always understand what was being suggested to him when members of his family suggested taking him on outings. Showing him a photograph of his potential destinations overcame this.

3. Use the photograph as a visual cue to support what is being said.

   For example, Sarah (page 19) did not know whom to expect to see when she returned to the home from her school. Staff used photographs when explaining to Sarah who was on duty: 'John is "on" tonight, Sarah [show photograph of John]. You like John, don't you?'

4. Use the photograph to help someone to discriminate one thing from another and thereby choose which they would like to have or do.

5. Where appropriate, build a collection of photographs to illustrate a journey (Bill, page 58), help to resolve loss (Les, page 23) or record an enriching experience (Patrick, page 45).

6. Keep the photographs as a record of experience and achievement, they will help to illustrate the achievements and potential of people to learn and grow.

Remember: photography should be seen as a creative adjunct to good care and training programmes. It can only support good assessment, action and evaluation which needs to be undertaken in

a global way, taking into account all the complexities that surround people in everyday life.

Some Important Points to Remember

- Ask permission before you take anyone's photograph.

- Be ready to discuss any reservations and ethical issues that may arise when you are taking photographs.

- Bear in mind that at any stage of a care plan or behaviour programme, specialist help may need to be sought.

- If your client exhibits a behavioural problem, ensure that all physical needs have been met and that a full assessment has been carried out.

- Take care to present photographs in the correct sequence and in steps or stages appropriate to that persons current ability.

- Revise the sequence and amount of photographs used in keeping as your client's knowledge and abilities develop.

- Change the photographs used if a new situation or area is introduced.

- A choice between just two photographs (options) may be a starting place for most people.

- Ensure that choices are acted upon immediately.

- Be conscious of the need to move forward, and when appropriate assist your client in applying his/her learning more generally.

- Always share with the person as well as those involved in the persons care, the use of photography and the importance of continuity and consistency of approach.

- Include all the photographs you have used in a teaching programme in any evaluation process.

- Praise and encourage when and where appropriate.

- Be patient. People will behave differently when a camera is first pointed at them.

- Try and show the subject matter clearly in your photographs. Avoid clutter and irrelevant objects or people. Ask yourself what you want your client to see.

- Protect photographs by using a clear plastic covering or placing them in an album.

- Keep negatives safe – you never know when you may need them again.

- Keep photographs up-to-date and replace any that become well-worn.

- Insure your camera.